EDITED BY HELEN EXLEY

Published in 2019 by Helen Exley®LONDON in Great Britain.
Illustration by Juliette Clarke © Helen Exley Creative Ltd 2019.
All the words by Pamela Dugdale, Odile Dormeuil, Hannah C.
Klein, Dalton Exley, Linda Gibson, Helen Exley, Charlotte Gray,
Mathilde and Sébastian Forestier, Pam Brown, Helen Thomson,
Stuart & Linda Macfarlane © Helen Exley Creative Ltd 2019.
Design, selection and arrangement © Helen Exley Creative Ltd 2019.
The moral right of the author has been asserted.

ISBN 978-1-78485-204-7

12 11 10 9 8 7 6 5 4 3 2 1

OTHER BOOKS IN THE SERIES

THE LITTLE BOOK OF *Gratitude*
THE LITTLE BOOK OF *Happiness*
THE LITTLE BOOK OF *Hope*
THE LITTLE BOOK OF *Kindness*

Helen Exley®LONDON
16 Chalk Hill, Watford, Herts WD19 4BG, UK
www.helenexley.com

THE LITTLE BOOK OF
Smiles

Helen Exley

...smiles
are all you
really need
sometimes.

ANGELINA JOLIE

THINGS THAT MAKE YOU SMILE

Walking in the country, after a shower
of snow has fallen makes me smile.
Sighting a robin singing happily to himself,
upon a snowy branch reminds me of other
people's happiness too. Bright parcels
makes me think of all the people who
have thought of me and bought gifts for me.
Watching a little child undoing a parcel
and seeing his eyes light up like little stars
when he reveals the gift from its wrapping
makes me smile.

CATHERINE POTTER, AGE 14

Even with her face a-twist,
I saw Someone peeking through.
And when Someone's nose was kissed,
Guess who came out giggling – YOU!

JOHN CIARDI

Smiles stitch the

world together.

PAM BROWN

Smile in the mirror.
Do that every morning
and you'll start to see a big difference
in your life.

YOKO ONO

Smiles reach the hard-to-reach places.

STEVE WILSON

We smile in sympathy, in greeting,
in apology, and in appreciation.
It is without doubt
the most important social bonding signal
in the human gestural repertoire.

DESMOND MORRIS

Today began dismally.
But all my worries disappeared
when someone smiled at me.

AUTHOR UNKNOWN

All people smile in the same language.

PROVERB

It costs nothing to say a "hello"
here and there.
To friends that you pass in the street.
It costs nothing to smile at a stranger,
Or any new friend that you meet.
It costs nothing to show your emotions,
or your feelings when things don't go right.
It costs nothing to help the unfortunate,
Who are blind or who have no sight.
It costs nothing to be happy.
And happiness can be found.
Happiness is like butter,
So go on and spread some around.

JEANETTE ACHILLES, AGE 15

…the effect of seeing a child's smile
compared to the same stimulation
which would be had from eating
2,000 chocolate bars
or receiving £16,000 in cash.

RESEARCH BY HEWLETT PACKARD

It takes just seventeen muscles to smile
but forty-three to frown.
So do what you've got to do with a smile
and it will take much less effort.

STUART & LINDA MACFARLANE

A dull drab day
and suddenly a little shaft of sun
and the face begins to thaw
and crack and crease
– and you are smiling.

ODILE DORMEUIL

Beauty breaks out everywhere –
in the smile on an aged face and on
the timeless tracks of the countryside.

AUTHOR UNKNOWN

Just one smile, immensely increases
the beauty of the universe.

SRI CHINMOY

Smiling is

nfectious.

BILL CULLEN

The happiness of life is made up of minute fractions – the little soon-forgotten charities of a kiss, a smile, a kind look, a heartfelt compliment in the disguise of a playful raillery, and the countless other infinitesimals of pleasant thought and feeling.

SAMUEL TAYLOR COLERIDGE

Smiles light up the shanty towns,
the slums and poorest villages.

JENNY DE VRIES

It is the small, insignificant,
simple gestures that make life bearable.
A smile, a touch, a word,
a kindness, a concern.

PAM BROWN

The more serious the face,
the more beautiful the smile.

FRANCOIS RENE DE CHATEAUBRIAND

A smile can say
"You are not alone.
If you need me, I am here."

ODILE DORMEUIL

Laughter is the sensation
of feeling good all over and showing it
principally in one place.

JOSH BILLINGS

The beauty of a smile, a smile of love
and compassion – that is never lost.

HELEN EXLEY

When feeling at your weakest you
end up showing more strength,
when at your lowest are suddenly
lifted above higher than you've ever been.
They all border one another, those opposites,
and how quickly we can be altered.
Despair can be altered by one simple smile
offered by a stranger.

CECILIA AHERN

A grin is a smile that invites you
to grin back.

PAMELA DUGDALE

Remember this:
every time we laugh,
we take a kink out of
the chain of life.

JOSH BILLINGS

Some people are too tired to give you a smile

Give them one of yours

As none needs a smile

So much as he who has no more to give.

AUTHOR UNKNOWN

...her smile was like a rainbow after a sudden storm.

SIDONIE GABRIELLE COLETTE

For me, human beings' ability to smile
is one of our most beautiful characteristics.
It is something no animal can do.
Not dogs, nor even whales or dolphins,
each of them very intelligent beings
with a clear affinity for humans,
can smile as we do.

THE DALAI LAMA

...smiles and kindness given habitually
are what win and preserve the heart.

SIR HUMPHREY DAVY

A friend of mine came over
and we talked about this life,
the happiness of laughter
and the foolishness of strife.
How much it means to face the world
with faith and courage true, to undertake
a certain task and really see it through.
And how unfortunate it is to sorrow
and despair and not to have the confidence

to conquer everywhere.

We said some people do not see

the comfort they could find,

if they would only try to smile and leave

their tears behind.

And then we wished with all our hearts

that we could find a way, to show the world

the wisdom of a smile for every day.

JAMES J. METCALFE

No matter how grouchy
you're feeling,
You'll find the smile
more or less healing.
It grows in a wreath
All around the front teeth -
Thus preserving the face
from congealing.

ANTHONY EUWER

Smile with relief.
Smile with satisfaction.
Smile with affection.
Smile with amusement.
Smile to find that life is good.

PAMELA DUGDALE

Make someone smile whenever
you can, you never know how much
of a difference you could be making
in their life at that moment.

AUTHOR UNKNOWN

It's something that makes you happy
in the house, spells goodwill in business,
takes up just a moment of time and stops
anybody being sad.
It's like sunshine when you're down,
it costs nothing to buy, no electricity
to operate, never loses power
if topped up and makes you happy
when repeated.
Yes, that's right – a smile!

FROM "THE FRIENDSHIP BOOK
OF FRANCIS GAY"

A frown can
sour a dozen's
people's day.
A smile
can set them
dancing.

ODILE DORMEUIL

If someone is courteous or does something
for you, however small,
whether you know them or not,
smile and thank them.
It's as good to receive, just as it is to give.

DALTON EXLEY

A smile is the best

f thank yous.

PAMELA DUGDALE

A smile is the light in your window
that tells others there is a caring,
sharing person inside.

AUTHOR UNKNOWN

I love smiles, and my wish is to see more smiles, real smiles, for there are many kinds – sarcastic, artificial, or diplomatic. Some smiles don't arouse any satisfaction, and some even engender suspicion or fear. An authentic smile, though, arouses an authentic feeling of freshness, and I think the smile belongs only to human beings.
If we want those smiles, we must create the reasons that make them appear.

THE DALAI LAMA

It is a terrible thing, this kindness
that human beings do not lose.
Terrible because when we are finally naked
in the dark and cold,
it is all we have.
We who are so rich, so full of strength,
we end up with that small change.
We have nothing else to give.

URSULA K. LE GUIN

Smile easily.
Laugh easily.
(You'll be dead all too soon
so you might as well laugh!).

DALTON EXLEY

Things are going wrong.
You feel low, a failure…
SMILE! Bare your teeth
if you can't smile from inside.
Fake it if you have to.
Everyone you see will feel better —
and so will you.

JODIE "BUBBLES" ALAN

Do what makes you happy,
be with who makes you smile,
laugh as much as you breathe,
and love as long as you live.

RACHEL ANN NUNES

When there are no smiles
despair has taken hold.
And we must bring them back.

JENNY DE VRIES

A smile creates
Happiness in the home,
It brings rest to the weary,
Best antidote for trouble.
It cannot be bought, begged,
Borrowed, or stolen, for it is
Something that is of no value
To anyone until it is given away.

AUTHOR UNKNOWN

Share your smile with the world.
It's a symbol of friendship and peace.

CHRISTIE BRINKLEY

...the most beautiful
smiles in the world
are the ones
that struggle
through the tears.

FROM "THE FRIENDSHIP BOOK
OF FRANCIS GAY"

A smile starts on the lips,
A grin spreads to the eyes,
A chuckle comes from the belly;
but a good laugh bursts forth
from the soul,
Overflows,
and bubbles all around.

CAROLYN BIRMINGHAM

It sounds like such a little thing to do,
but say "Thank You" a lot. With a big smile.

DALTON EXLEY

A small smile
from the person at the till,
or the bus driver.
A friendly word
from the library assistant.
A cheerful exchange.
A civil garage attendant.
And that moment,
the day is changed.
One's hope in all humanity is restored!

ODILE DORMEUIL

Wear a smile. One

ize fits all.

While you are fighting and struggling with your enemy, if you smile, naturally your enemy will lose some of its strength. So play a trick on your enemy by smiling. This may sound absurd, but I assure you it is true. Just think of the negativity-world as an enemy whose strength can be weakened by your smile.

SRI CHINMOY

Smile when picking up the phone;
the caller will hear it in your voice.

ANTHONY ROBBINS

The gentler the smile, the more
powerful the comfort.

JENNY DE VRIES

A strange country.
A strange language.
But you are met with smiles.
You are welcome.
You are home.

PAMELA DUGDALE

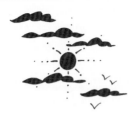

However drab the day.
You smile and the
sun breaks through.

HANNAH C. KLEIN

Pack for a change of weather.

Pack a paperback.

Pack a quantity of smiles.

Particularly if you haven't the language.

PAM BROWN

smile (n.)
the shortest distance
between two people.

A rose spreads its scent
and makes me smile.
A person spreads their love
and makes the whole world smile.

LINDA GIBSON

You know when someone unexpectedly smiles at you, it makes you smile doesn't it. And for a precious moment you are happy. No need to think about why, it just happens.
A lovely free gift of life.
So go on, don't be mean, don't hoard your smiles, share them, share a little happiness.

DALTON EXLEY

I had discovered true love.
The love which repays slavery and exhaustion with a brief smile. But what a smile!

SUE LIMB

Overcome shyness. Say "Hello" to everyone you meet. Smile at everybody! You'll be so surprised, people won't think you're stark raving mad. They'll like it!

HAROLD ALTDON

Someone is singing out of happiness and the world about them smiles.

PAM BROWN

Even if we spend a lot of money on gifts
for everyone in our family, nothing we buy
could give them as much happiness
as the gift of our awareness, our smile.

THICH NHAT HANH

Happiness is internal. A smile also
makes it external. So smile – it makes
the world so much happier.

STUART & LINDA MACFARLANE

A smile among
dark frowns:
a beloved light:
A solitude,
a refuge,
a delight.

PERCY BYSSHE SHELLEY

M ay no one ever come to you
without going away better and happier.
Everyone should see kindness in your face,
in your eyes, in your smile.

MOTHER TERESA

O ne lonely person.
One other lonely person.
One shy smile.
One friendly grin.
Two happy people.

HELEN EXLEY

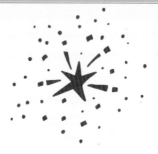

Waht is it that may relieve a situation
of stress and pain or which has the power
to make a friend? No one is so poor
that he has no need of it.
No one is so rich that he or she cannot
share it. A smile appears in the dictionary
as a facial expression in which corners
of the mouth curve upwards,
expressing joy and pleasure.

AUTHOR UNKNOWN

Learn to greet your friends with a smile;
They carry too many frowns
in their own hearts
to be bothered with yours.

MARY ALLETTE AYER

More smiling, less worrying.
More compassion, less judgment.
More blessed, less stressed.
More love, less hate.

ROY T. BENNETT

Every smile
makes the world
more beautiful.

HELEN THOMSON

Maman told me that every time you smile, a very tiny bit of the smile stays stuck to your face, so as you get older and older your face starts to show all the tiny bits of all your smiles and you look like you are smiling all the time, even when you are just thinking about what to have for breakfast. She said, also, that if you frown a lot then the frown sticks to your face instead. That way when you are old you have a very frowny face and look cross all the time and people are scared of you.

CLAIRE KING

He is seven years old
and he is beaming, his crooked tooth
exposed in a smile as wide as his
outstretched arms.
His huge brown eyes sunk deep
into his face tell of the suffering
he must have endured since
his world came crashing down
on him eight days earlier,
but the smile overshadows everything.

JOHN HUMPHRYS

Actions speak louder than words,
and a smile says, "I like you.
You make me happy.
I am glad to see you."

DALE CARNEGIE

The best smile of all
is a baby's smile.
It has no guile or
calculation.
It is pure joy.

PAM BROWN

Too often we underestimate
the power of a touch,
a smile, a kind word,
a listening ear,
an honest compliment,
or the smallest act of caring,
all of which have the potential
to turn a life around.

LEO BUSCAGLIA

A smile enriches those who receive
Without making poorer those who give.
It takes but a moment,
But the memory of it sometimes
Lasts forever.
None is so rich or mighty that
They can get along without it,
And none is so poor but that
They can be made rich by it.

AUTHOR UNKNOWN

Bad days are just good days where you forgot to smile.

STUART & LINDA MACFARLANE

Weep if you must, but always, always make a point of starting and finishing every day with a smile.

AUTHOR UNKNOWN

Scientists inform us coldly
that a smile is merely the movement
of thirteen muscles,
while a frown, it seems, requires
fifty muscles.
But the fact remains that a frown
is very depressing
while the small amount of effort
to produce a smile works wonders.

GAIA

Breathe in, smile, breathe out. Be at peace. . .

HELEN EXLEY

To offer friendship.
To disarm suspicion.
To show gratitude.
To calm the antagonist.
To share a joy.
So small a thing,
and yet so powerful.

PAMELA DUGDALE

You're never fully dressed without
a smile.

MARTIN CHARNIN

Change your habits totally.
In everything you do give up negativity,
thank people, laugh, give compliments.
Every day, every hour,
Smile. Smile. Smile.

DALTON EXLEY

Too often people don't understand
the power of a smile.
Each one of us has the power to turn
a life around.

AUTHOR UNKNOWN

The sleepy smile crowns the long and happy day.

MAYA V. PATEL

The powerful emotions triggered
when someone important
in our lives smiles at us and
we smile back changes our
brain chemistry.
It creates a 'halo' effect
that helps us remember other
happy events more vividly,
feel more optimistic,
more positive and more motivated.

DR. DAVID LEWIS

When a group of refugees arrived
in an English town a welcome gathering
was laid on. As one woman spoke
to the newcomers in their own tongue
and others plied them with tea and scones,
an elderly disabled woman said,
"I'm so sorry. I can't do anything for them."
"Yes, you can," said one of the organisers.
"You can smile."

FROM "THE FRIENDSHIP BOOK
OF FRANCIS GAY"

We can offer a wide range of smiles.
All guaranteed
and to be had in great variety.
The gentle smile is popular.
But then, there is the beam,
the grin.
The generous or restrained.
The provocative. The sympathetic.
The complacent.
The flirtatious.
The courageous.

The manly and the motherly.

The condescending.

The superior.

Apologetic or dubious.

Conspiratorial.

Placating.

Or affectionate.

Keep a selection to hand.

You never know

when you will need one.

PAM BROWN

When life gives you a hundred reasons
to cry, show life that you have a thousand
reasons to smile.

AUTHOR UNKNOWN

Running can benefit the body –
swimming can benefit the body.
But there is one exercise that is more
important and should be practiced
at every opportunity – smiling.

STUART & LINDA MACFARLANE

The sound of laughter has always seemed to me the most civilized music in the universe.

SIR PETER USTINOV

When we thank people it makes them smile and that usually makes us smile too. Spread a little sunshine!

DALTON EXLEY

Smiles between strangers hold the world together.

CHARLOTTE GRAY

One day most of the family
was together in the mailroom,
busily sorting through stacks of letters.
Will was on the floor playing.
He looked up and said, "Mommy,
Daddy can't move his arms anymore."
Dana said, "That's right,
Daddy can't move his arms."

"And Daddy can't run around anymore."
"That's right; he can't run around anymore."
"And Daddy can't talk."
Then Will paused, screwed up his face
in concentration, and burst out happily,
"But he can still smile."
Everyone put down what they were doing
and just looked at one another.

CHRISTOPHER REEVE

To stay sane in the world today
it is imperative to daily
do something daft and raise a smile.

CHARLOTTE GRAY

Smiling helps you
approach the day
with gentleness and
understanding.

THICH NHAT HANH

If you don't have
a big smile to give
a very, very
small one will do.

HELEN EXLEY

A smile is a gentle thing –
can be offered quietly
– an offer of friendship.
Understood by every human creature.

PAMELA DUGDALE

...smiling is the biggest and best beauty secret.

NORMANDIE KEITH

Someone smiles at you.
Smile back,
however great the effort.
You'll find it spreads
and warms your eyes and ears and nose,
your finger tips and toes.

ODILE DORMEUIL

Wear a smile and have friends;
wear a scowl and have wrinkles.

LEO BUSCAGLIA

At what are we smiling?
We don't know, and we don't care.
We are communicating with one another
in happiness, and the smiles are the outward
display of our delight and our love.

JOAN LOWERY NIXON

So many currencies.
Sterling. Euro. Dollar. Yen.
A world divided.
And yet a smile's accepted anywhere.
Recognised. Accepted.
Welcome.

PAM BROWN

How rich we are if we can give
friendship, a smile, a handshake,
encouragement, good cheer, sympathy.
These are gifts indeed.

FROM "THE FRIENDSHIP BOOK
OF FRANCIS GAY"

Some people have a beautiful smile
and when people see it they feel happy.

SUSANNAH MORRIS, AGE 10

The human race has only one
really effective weapon
and that is laughter.
Against the assault of laughter
nothing can stand.

MARK TWAIN

Some of the most common ideas
for spreading happiness are simple things
like smiling, saying thank you, giving time
or listening to another person and always
being positive. Try to make these habits
of a lifetime. But imagine if you developed
the one simple habit of smiling at people –
for the rest of your life.
That would mean that you spread happiness
wherever you go. Awesome!

HELEN EXLEY

Smiling people are like sunshine, they will always bring happiness wherever they go.

AUTHOR UNKNOWN

Positivity, happiness, kindness and smiles are infectious! Start an outbreak!

DALTON EXLEY

Wrinkles should merely indicate where smiles have been.

MARK TWAIN

A single smile...
could travel
round the earth.

BILL CULLEN

So, if you feel a smile begin, don't leave it
undetected, let's start an epidemic quick,
and get the world infected.

RUSSELL H. CONWELL

Whap children are looking for is a hug,
a lap, a kind word, a touch,
someone to read them a story,
somebody to smile and share with.

JOHN THOMPSON

A Child of Happiness always seems
like an old soul living in a new body,
and her face is very serious until she smiles,
and then the sun lights up the world....

ANNE CAMERON

Wake up with
a smile – make
this the best day
of your life.

STUART & LINDA MACFARLANE

The real pauper
is the person
without a smile.

MATHILDE AND SÉBASTIEN FORESTIER

If somebody apologizes to you,
accept it gracefully.
With a smile. Life is short.

DALTON EXLEY

Keep smiling,
because life is a beautiful thing and there's so much to smile about.

MARILYN MONROE

Strong people are ones who can smile for others' happiness.

VERONICA PURCELL

A smile acts as an escape from loneliness.

AUTHOR UNKNOWN

Every child in
the world should
be able to smile -
we owe it to them,
each and every one.

CHARLOTTE GRAY

The shortest
distance between
two people
is a long and
happy smile.

VICTOR BORGE

Nothing is more
beautiful than
cheerfulness
in an old face.

JEAN PAUL RICHTER

The strong person smiles in trouble,
gathers strength from distress,
and grows brave by reflection.

THOMAS PAINE

We're all in the same boat, we humans.
Worries over bills and children.
Illness. Trouble with the car.
Any small friendly gesture
– a smile, a hand with the luggage,
a door held open – says we understand.
We're family.

MAYA V. PATEL

Smile at strangers
and you just might change a life.

STEVE MARABOLI

Be happy in the moment, that's enough.
Each moment is all we need, not more.
Be happy now and if you show through
your actions that you love others,
including those who are poorer
than you, you'll give them happiness too.
It doesn't take much –
it can be just giving a smile.
The world would be a much better place
if everyone smiled more.
So smile, be cheerful.

MOTHER TERESA

Those who bring sunshine to the lives of others cannot keep it from themselves.

SIR JAMES M. BARRIE

Most often, you won't know
what happened because of your smile...
But you won't know what happened
all the times that you scowl,
that you are preoccupied –
or simply don't care.

AUTHOR UNKNOWN

You are not fully dressed
until you put a smile on.

EVAN ESAR

What sunshine
is to flowers,
smiles are
to humanity.

JOSEPH ADDISON